**This book belongs to:**

_____

&

_____

# Before You

# Before You

A Book by Me, Your Parent, from a
Time When You Didn't Exist

QUIRK BOOKS

PHILADELPHIA

Library of Congress Control Number: 2023932030

ISBN: 978-1-68369-377-2

Printed in China

Typeset in Etna and Freight Sans

Designed by Elissa Flanigan
Production management by John J. McGurk
Text by Jess Zimmerman

Quirk Books
215 Church Street
Philadelphia, PA 19106
quirkbooks.com

10 9 8 7 6 5 4 3 2 1

# Contents

# To the Author

Most of this book is for your future kid. But this introduction is for you, the parent-to-be and author-to-be. So if you're a kid and you're reading this section, you can stop, because it's about to get boring for kids!

Are the kids gone? Great. The first thing we need to establish is that microeconomics focuses on the behavior of individual agents such as consumers and businesses, whereas macroeconomics looks at decision matrices of those agents and the aggregate effects of resultant behavior patterns.

Okay, now they're really gone. Listen, here's the tea: in the very near future, you're facing a big change in how others see you (and how you see yourself). Right now you know yourself as an individual, with likes and dislikes and pet peeves and priorities and personal traumas and coping strategies and personality traits and a first name. But for the next few years, that person may feel very distant, even imaginary. You'll spend much of your time being someone named Mama or Dada or whatever term of address you choose, and a lot of people—especially, for a while, your kid—will forget that you're anything else.

It's fine! None of this is bad, and even if it's challenging, it'll be outweighed by all the positive parts of parenting. But the last thing you need is another baby book or journal reinforcing the idea that the most important thing about you is your kid. You already know your kid is important! You are about to voluntarily allow them to take over your life, and what's more, you're going to love it! But what you might forget, for a little while, is that you're important too. You're a real, whole, independent individual, and that's not going to change. Recording what that person is like right now will make it easier to remember and keep hold of them, even when they feel like a mirage.

That's not selfish. Quite the opposite, actually. When your kid is a little older, it's also going to be really good for them to understand that their parent is a person: someone who had a whole life before they came along, someone who has feelings and makes mistakes just like them. The goal of this book is to help you document your pre-baby self, so you can share that person with your kid.

You'll be talking to your child-to-be throughout the book, filling them in on what you were like when you were a kid and what you're like right now. It may be tricky to figure out how to talk to them, since they don't exist yet. So before you start, take a moment to picture your kid sometime in the future, when they're old enough to read. Think about what they might look like, what they might care about, what they might worry about. Imagine them as a real, whole person, with likes and dislikes, anxieties and interests. A fully realized individual.

Just like you.

# To the Reader

*This is a space for you to write an introductory note to your future child.*

# 1.

# Way Before You

Way, way back before you were born, I used to be a kid too! I was a lot like you in some ways, and in other ways I was totally different (especially because it was kind of a long time ago, and because being a kid was different then). Here's some stuff that was definitely the same: I had a head and a body and I lived on Earth! Also, I had a family, and I spent my days learning things and having fun, and I had a lot of feelings. Do you think I had the same family as you, learned the same things, had fun the same way, and had the same feelings? Let's find out what all of that was like way before you!

Here's a drawing or photo of me
when I was a kid:

# At Home

Think about where we live now. What does our home look like? How big is it? Who lives here with you? What's your favorite room, and what do you like most about it? When I was your age, I lived in **a different house / a different state / a different country** (circle one)! But just like you, I shared my home with people I loved (and who sometimes got on my nerves). I had favorite special places, and maybe even secret hideouts! Here's what the place I lived was like way before you.

☐ I lived in the same home the whole time I was a kid.

☐ I lived in more than one home.

Here are some places I lived and my age when I lived there:

_____

_____

_____

_____

_____

_____

_____

_____

_____

_____

_____

_____

_____

_____

_____

_____

_____

_____

_____

We had _____ kids in our home and _____ adults.

The kids who lived with me were named:

_____

_____

_____

_____

_____

_____

_____

_____

_____

_____

_____

The adults who lived with me were named:

_____

_____

_____

_____

_____

_____

_____

_____

_____

_____

_____

My favorite thing about **having / not having** (circle one) siblings was:

_____

_____

_____

_____

_____

_____

_____

☐ I got along well with the adults in my house.

☐ I had a hard time sometimes with my adults.

The thing I most loved doing with my adults was:

_____

_____

_____

_____

_____

_____

_____

_____

_____

_____

One thing we did every day was:

_____

_____

_____

_____

_____

_____

_____

_____

_____

_____

But on special days we would:

_____

_____

_____

_____

_____

_____

_____

_____

_____

_____

_____

My favorite thing we would eat for dinner was:

_____

_____

_____

_____

But my *least* favorite thing we would eat for dinner was:

_____

_____

_____

_____

Here's what we would have had for dinner if I was in charge:

_____

_____

_____

Here are some of my other favorite foods from childhood:

_____

_____

_____

_____

_____

_____

_____

☐ I had _____ real pets.

☐ I had _____ imaginary pets.

Here's more about the pets I had or wished I had:

_____

_____

_____

_____

_____

_____

_____

_____

_____

_____

_____

_____

_____

_____

_____

☐ I helped take care of my pet or pets.
My job was:

_____

_____

☐ I let other people take care of them.

☐ Sometimes I got in trouble.

☐ I never got in trouble.

☐ Okay, fine, I *rarely* got in trouble.

I was most likely to get in trouble for:

_____
_____
_____
_____
_____
_____
_____

The biggest thing I got in trouble for was:

_____
_____
_____
_____
_____
_____
_____

☐ I'm sorry I did it.

☐ I'd do it again.

Here's a description of my room growing up:

_____
_____
_____
_____
_____
_____
_____

My favorite thing about it was:

_____
_____
_____
_____
_____
_____
_____

But what I didn't like was:

_____
_____
_____
_____
_____
_____
_____

My favorite place in the house or neighborhood was:

_____

_____

_____

_____

_____

_____

_____

I liked it because:

_____

_____

_____

_____

_____

_____

_____

When I was there I liked to:

_____

_____

_____

_____

_____

_____

_____

☐ I had a secret hideout in my house or neighborhood.

Here's what it was like:

_____

_____

_____

_____

_____

_____

_____

_____

_____

☐ I didn't have a secret hideout.

Here's what I imagine it would have been like if I had one:

_____

_____

_____

_____

_____

_____

_____

_____

_____

Here's a drawing I made of the perfect room
or hideout for a kid like me!

# My School

Everyone who's a kid has to learn stuff, although our schools might not look the same and we don't always learn the same things. My school was pretty different from yours because I went to school such a long time ago, so paper and books hadn't been invented and we had to write on rocks and ride a dinosaur instead of a school bus! Okay, okay, I'm just kidding—here's what my school was really like way before you.

Here are the schools I went to and how old I was when I went there:

_____

_____

_____

_____

_____

_____

_____

_____

_____

_____

_____

_____

_____

☐ I liked going to school.

☐ I didn't like going to school.

☐ I would have rather:

_____

_____

☐ Actually, I did my learning at home so I didn't go anywhere.

My favorite subject in school was:

_____

_____

_____

_____

_____

But I wasn't such a big fan of:

_____

_____

_____

_____

My favorite teacher was:

_____

_____

_____

_____

- ☐ I always did my homework.

- ☐ I never did my homework.

- ☐ I sometimes did my homework.

- ☐ Nobody even tried to give me homework!

☐ I did other activities at school:

☐ School sports.
Sports played:

_____

_____

_____

_____

☐ School clubs.
Club names:

_____

_____

_____

_____

☐ Extra classes:

_____

_____

_____

_____

☐ Something else:

_____

_____

_____

_____

☐ I didn't do other activities at school.

The coolest thing I learned in school was:

_____
_____
_____
_____
_____
_____
_____
_____
_____
_____

One important thing I learned about school was:

_____
_____
_____
_____
_____
_____
_____
_____
_____
_____
_____
_____

My favorite thing to do during the school year was:

_____

_____

_____

_____

_____

_____

_____

My favorite thing to do in summer was:

_____

_____

_____

_____

_____

_____

_____

☐ I went to summer day camp.

☐ I went to summer sleepaway camp.

☐ I didn't go to summer camp.

# Having Fun

I bet sometimes you think I hate to have fun, because it's my job to tell you that you have to go to school, or you're not allowed to eat candy for dinner, or we can't have an alligator for a pet. Surprise: I actually love to have fun, and when I was a kid I did it all the time! (Back then it was someone else's job to tell me to go to school.) The things I did for fun then were different than they are now, and maybe different from what you do for fun, but just like you I had friends, toys, and favorite hobbies. Here's what I used to do for fun way before you.

☐ I liked to play imagination games.

☐ I liked to play with toys.

☐ I liked to play board games and card games.

☐ I liked to play computer games and video games.

My favorite thing to play was:

_____

_____

_____

_____

_____

_____

_____

_____

I did *not* like to play:

_____

_____

_____

_____

_____

_____

_____

_____

_____

My best friend was named:

_____

☐  We're still friends!

☐  We stayed friends until:

_____

_____

Here's how we met:

_____
_____
_____
_____
_____
_____
_____
_____
_____
_____
_____
_____
_____
_____
_____
_____
_____

My favorite thing about my best friend was:

_____
_____
_____
_____
_____
_____
_____
_____
_____
_____
_____

Our favorite thing to do together was:

_____
_____
_____
_____
_____
_____
_____
_____
_____
_____
_____
_____
_____

Some of my other important friends were named:

_____

_____

_____

_____

_____

_____

_____

_____

_____

_____

_____

We liked to:

☐ Play games or sports.

☐ Play with toys.

☐ Build or make things.

☐ Have parties.

☐ Watch TV or movies.

☐ Eat snacks.

☐ Something else: _____

Here's a story about something fun I did with one or more friends:

_____

_____

_____

_____

_____

_____

_____

_____

_____

_____

_____

_____

_____

_____

_____

_____

_____

_____

_____

_____

_____

_____

_____

_____

I really loved to:

☐ Read.
Favorite books:

_____

_____

_____

_____

☐ Watch TV.
Favorite shows:

_____

_____

_____

_____

☐ Watch movies.
Favorite movies:

_____

_____

_____

_____

☐ Make things.
Favorite crafts or projects:

_____

_____

_____

_____

☐ Listen to music.
Favorite songs or albums:

_____

_____

_____

_____

☐ Play games.
Favorite games:

_____

_____

_____

_____

☐ Play sports.
Favorite sports:

_____

_____

_____

_____

☐ Something else:

_____

_____

_____

_____

_____

_____

_____

My favorite place to go was:

_____

_____

When I was there I would:

_____

_____

_____

_____

_____

_____

_____

_____

_____

_____

_____

_____

_____

_____

_____

_____

_____

Here's some other stuff I did to have fun that I haven't mentioned yet:

# My Feelings

I probably hurt your feelings sometimes (only ever by accident, though!), or I might do things that make you frustrated or mad, and you may think that I don't know what it feels like to be a kid. If you think this, you're a little bit right, because it was a long time ago for me, and also my grown-up feelings aren't exactly the same as my kid feelings. (I'll tell you more about that later!) But when I think about it, I do remember the feelings I had when I was your age and what I did about them. Here's some feelings I used to have way before you.

Here's something that always made me happy:

_____

_____

_____

_____

_____

_____

When I was happy I wanted to:

_____

_____

_____

_____

_____

I was especially proud of:

_____

_____

_____

_____

_____

_____

When I was proud I wanted to:

_____

_____

_____

_____

I was really scared of:

_____

_____

_____

_____

_____

_____

I **am / am not** (circle one) still scared of it.

Sometimes I was so scared I would:

_____

_____

_____

_____

_____

_____

One important thing I learned about being scared was:

_____

_____

_____

_____

_____

_____

Sometimes I got sad! Here's something that used to make me sad:

_____
_____
_____
_____
_____

When I was sad I would:

_____
_____
_____
_____
_____

I always felt less sad when:

_____
_____
_____
_____
_____

One important thing I learned about being sad was:

_____
_____
_____
_____
_____

Sometimes I got mad or frustrated! Here's something I used to get mad about:

_____

_____

_____

_____

When I was mad I would:

_____

_____

_____

_____

_____

I always felt less mad when:

_____

_____

_____

_____

_____

One important thing I learned about being mad was:

_____

_____

_____

_____

_____

Here's a story about a time I had a really big feeling and what I did about it:

_____

_____

_____

_____

_____

_____

_____

_____

_____

_____

_____

_____

_____

_____

_____

_____

_____

_____

_____

_____

_____

_____

_____

_____

_____

_____

_____

_____

# The First Time I . . .

The coolest (and maybe the toughest) thing about being a kid is that you get to do so many things you've never done before. That can be exciting because you're having new experiences, but also a little scary because you're not sure what to expect. I've had a lot of chances to get comfortable and familiar with stuff since I was a kid, although I still get to do things I've never tried before—you never have to stop trying new things if you don't want to! But before I could practice things and get good at them, I had to do them for the first time. Here's what that was like for me, way before you.

The first time I won something was:

_____

_____

_____

_____

_____

It made me feel:

_____

_____

_____

_____

_____

Here's how it happened:

_____

_____

_____

_____

_____

_____

_____

_____

_____

_____

_____

_____

_____

The first time I spent the night away from home was:

_____

_____

_____

_____

It made me feel:

_____

_____

_____

_____

Here's how it happened:

_____

_____

_____

_____

_____

_____

_____

_____

_____

_____

_____

The first time I traveled somewhere was:

_____

_____

_____

_____

_____

It made me feel:

_____

_____

_____

_____

_____

Here's how it happened:

_____

_____

_____

_____

_____

_____

_____

_____

_____

_____

_____

_____

The first time I had a crush on someone was:

_____
_____
_____
_____

It made me feel:

_____
_____
_____
_____

Here's how it happened:

_____
_____
_____
_____
_____
_____
_____
_____
_____
_____
_____
_____

The first time I lived away from my family was:

_____

_____

_____

_____

_____

It made me feel:

_____

_____

_____

_____

Here's how it happened:

_____

_____

_____

_____

_____

_____

_____

_____

_____

_____

_____

_____

# More About Me Then

That's *most* of the things you need to know about what my life was like when I was a kid like you. But there are a few more important things I want you to know that didn't fit in any of the other categories. If you get to the end of this section and there's still more that you want to know about what it was like way before you, you can ask me anything!

When I grew up I wanted to become:

_____

_____

_____

_____

_____

Here's what I liked about that idea:

_____

_____

_____

_____

_____

_____

_____

_____

_____

_____

_____

_____

_____

_____

☐   And that's what I did!

☐   I did something different (I'll tell you about it later).

When I was a kid, my favorite holiday was:

_____

_____

_____

_____

Because:

_____

_____

_____

_____

_____

Here's how we celebrated in my family:

_____

_____

_____

_____

_____

_____

_____

_____

_____

_____

_____

The best costume I ever wore was:

_____

_____

_____

_____

Here's what it looked like:

Some stuff that's totally normal for you hadn't been invented yet when I was a kid!

We didn't have: _____

    Instead we: _____

We didn't have: _____

    Instead we: _____

We didn't have: _____

    Instead we: _____

Here's an idea I had for an invention. Maybe if *you* have kids, they'll think my invention is totally normal!

_____

_____

_____

_____

_____

_____

_____

_____

_____

Wait, there are some important things about me as a kid that I forgot to tell you! Here they are:

_____
_____
_____
_____
_____
_____
_____
_____
_____
_____
_____
_____
_____
_____
_____
_____
_____
_____
_____
_____
_____
_____
_____
_____
_____
_____

# 2.

# Right Before You

Now I'm a grown-up, and pretty soon I'm going to be your parent! When you get here you're going to need a whole lot of help and love and attention, and I'll spend a ton of time with you, but you won't be great at having a conversation right away. Someday, though, you'll be old enough that we'll be able to talk together about what we like and how we feel, and even the mistakes we make sometimes. (If you're reading this, that means *someday* is now!) I'll want to tell you what it feels like to be your parent, and what it was like to watch you grow—but I'll also want to tell you about who I am now and what life was like right before you.

Here's a drawing or photo of what
I look like right now:

# All About Me

You know (I hope!) that you're a special person, the only one like you in the entire world. Guess what: that's true about parents too! Everyone is different and special, and some of the things that make us unique are our interests, our skills, our likes and dislikes, the things we're proud of and the things we're not so proud of. Here are some facts about the special person I am, from right before you.

Here's some words I use to describe myself:

But if you asked people who know me really well,
they'd describe me with words like:

I'm especially proud of:

Don't tell anyone I'm embarrassed about:

Here's some stuff I like:

Get this stuff away from me, though:

I am really good at:

_____

_____

☐  I taught myself.

☐  I took lessons.

☐  I just realized I was good at it naturally.

I was _____ years old when I started learning or practicing it.

Here's how I practice:

_____

_____

_____

_____

_____

If you also want to be good at it, the most important thing you need to know is:

_____

_____

_____

_____

_____

I am not so good at:

_____

_____

☐ I want to get better at it.

☐ I don't care about getting better at it.

Here's something important I learned about being not so good at things:

_____

_____

_____

I wish I were good at:

_____

_____

☐ But getting good at it seems really hard.

☐ But it's pretty dangerous.

☐ But I have another reason:

_____

_____

_____

☐ Maybe I'll learn to get good at it someday!

# My Every Day

Think about our routine together. Where does our family live? What do we normally do in the mornings, or on weekends? What do we like to eat? Some of those things were the same before you, but others have changed a lot. A regular day with you looks way different than it did before! Here's what my regular days were like right before you.

I dress like this most of the time:

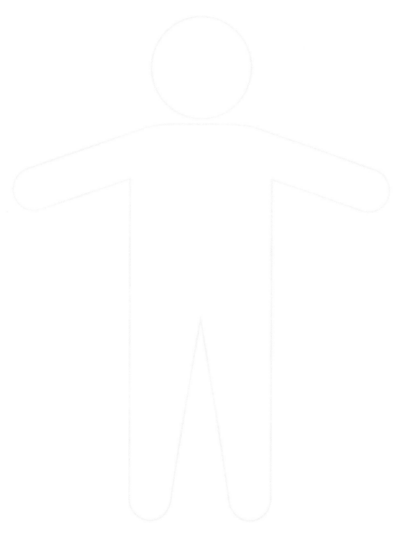

If you can't tell, I'm wearing:

_____
_____
_____
_____

I live in:

Neighborhood: _____

Town or city: _____

State or province: _____

Country: _____

Continent: _____

Planet: _____

☐ I live in a house.

☐ I live in an apartment.

☐ I live in a dorm room.

☐ I live in a temporary place like a hotel.

☐ I live in a cave.

☐ I live in: _____

☐ I live by myself for now (soon I'll live with you!).

☐ I live with someone else: _____

My favorite thing about where I live is:

_____
_____
_____
_____
_____
_____
_____
_____
_____

My least favorite thing about where I live is:

_____
_____
_____
_____
_____
_____
_____
_____
_____

I wake up at _____ o'clock.

I go to sleep at _____ o'clock.

☐   I usually have dreams.

☐   I don't usually have dreams (that I remember).

The weirdest dream I ever had was:

_____

_____

_____

_____

_____

_____

_____

_____

_____

_____

_____

_____

_____

_____

_____

For breakfast I usually have:

_____

_____

For lunch I usually have:

_____

_____

For dinner I usually have:

_____

_____

My very favorite thing to eat is:

_____

_____

_____

_____

_____

_____

☐ I'll make it for you!

☐ I'll get someone else to make it for you!

☐ I don't think you'd like it (but you can try!).

☐ It's not a food you can have, but maybe we can
come up with a new version.

☐ I have a pet.

☐ I have more than one pet.

☐ I don't have a pet.

☐ I want a pet.

Maybe someday we can get: _____

But please don't ask me for: _____

☐ I'm allergic.

☐ I'm scared of them.

☐ I don't think we have room.

☐ I just don't want one in the house.

☐ Another reason:

_____

_____

_____

_____

_____

_____

_____

My job is: _____

That means that most days I:

_____

_____

_____

_____

_____

_____

☐ I like my job most of the time.

☐ I like my job some of the time.

☐ I like my job a little of the time.

☐ I wish I were doing this instead:

_____

_____

I get to work by:

☐ Car.

☐ Foot.

☐ Bike.

☐ Public transportation (like bus or subway).

☐ Horse.

☐ Other: _____

☐ I work at my house, so I don't have to leave.

What I like about work:

_____

_____

_____

_____

What I don't like about work:

_____

_____

_____

_____

Maybe someday I will:

_____

_____

_____

_____

In my spare time I like to:

☐ Do arts and crafts.
   Favorite crafts:

_____

_____

☐ Watch TV or movies.
   Favorite shows or movies:

_____

_____

Play a sport.
Favorite sports:

_____

_____

Play a game.
Favorite games:

_____

_____

Listen to music.
Favorite songs or albums:

_____

_____

Do political activism.
For example:

_____

_____

Learn something.
Favorite subjects:

_____

_____

Something else:

_____

_____

# Exciting Times

Of course, I didn't just have regular days before you—I also had special days, like weekends and vacations and holidays. I know, it probably sounds wild that I had fun before you existed! How could that be possible? But believe it or not, I had some adventures and exciting times right before you.

On a normal weekend I like to:

_____

_____

_____

_____

_____

_____

_____

_____

_____

_____

_____

But my best weekend ever was when I:

_____

_____

_____

_____

_____

_____

_____

_____

_____

_____

_____

_____

I've visited these countries:

The coolest place I ever traveled to was:

_____
_____
_____
_____

The most fun thing I did there was:

_____
_____
_____
_____
_____
_____
_____
_____

The place I most want to travel is:

_____
_____
_____
_____

If I could live anywhere in the world it would be:

_____
_____
_____
_____

If I could do exactly what I wanted every day, I would:

If I could do exactly what I wanted for one day only,
I would:

My favorite holiday is: _____

Here's what I like about it:

_____
_____
_____
_____
_____
_____
_____
_____

Here's how I like to celebrate it:

_____
_____
_____
_____
_____
_____
_____
_____
_____
_____
_____
_____

My favorite season is:

☐ Spring.

☐ Summer.

☐ Fall.

☐ Winter.

Here's what I like best about it:

_____

_____

_____

_____

_____

_____

_____

_____

_____

_____

_____

_____

_____

_____

_____

My favorite thing to do in spring is:

My favorite thing to do in summer is:

My favorite thing to do in fall is:

My favorite thing to do in winter is:

☐ Sometimes I dress up.

☐ I almost never dress up.

Here's the fanciest outfit I ever wore:

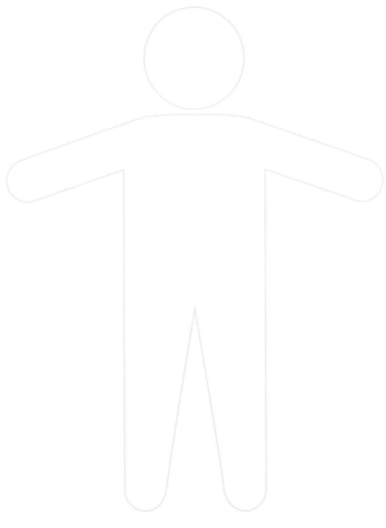

I wore it for: _____

Here's a drawing or photo of me doing
one of my favorite things:

# Grown-up Feelings

Think about what makes you scared, sad, happy, or mad. How do you handle those feelings? Who do you tell about them? Do the feelings sometimes seem so big that it's hard to know what to do? My grown-up feelings are different from my kid feelings, and yours will probably be different too. But all of us have feelings, and it's important to be able to understand and talk about them. Here are some of the ways and reasons I used to feel scared, sad, happy, or mad right before you.

One big thing that makes me happy is thinking about and planning for YOU! Here are some other things that make me happy:

Remember how I used to be scared of _____ ?
Well . . .

☐ I'm still scared of it.

☐ I'm still a *little* scared of it (but mostly not).

☐ I'm scared of a different thing now.

☐ Now I'm not scared of anything!

My biggest fear is:

_____

_____

_____

_____

_____

_____

_____

_____

_____

_____

_____

_____

_____

_____

_____

It's okay to be scared because:

_____

_____

_____

_____

_____

_____

_____

But if you want to learn to be brave, here's what you
need to know:

_____

_____

_____

_____

_____

_____

_____

_____

_____

_____

_____

_____

_____

Remember how _____ used to make me sad?

Here's something I get sad about now:

_____
_____
_____
_____
_____
_____
_____
_____
_____

When I'm sad I usually show it by:

_____
_____
_____
_____
_____
_____
_____
_____
_____
_____
_____
_____

I think the best thing to do when you're sad is:

_____

_____

_____

_____

_____

_____

_____

It's okay to be sad because:

_____

_____

_____

_____

_____

_____

_____

But when I'm ready to feel less sad, here's what I do:

_____

_____

_____

_____

_____

_____

_____

Remember how _____ used to make me mad?

Here's something that makes me mad now:

_____

_____

_____

_____

_____

_____

_____

_____

When I'm mad I usually show it by:

_____

_____

_____

_____

_____

_____

_____

_____

_____

_____

I think the best thing to do when you're mad is:

_____

_____

_____

_____

_____

_____

It's okay to be mad because:

_____

_____

_____

_____

_____

_____

_____

But when I'm ready to feel less mad, here's what I do:

_____

_____

_____

_____

_____

_____

Sometimes I worry about stuff, like:

_____

_____

_____

_____

_____

_____

_____

_____

_____

_____

When I get too worried, I try to:

_____

_____

_____

_____

_____

_____

_____

_____

_____

_____

_____

Sometimes I get nervous about problems in the world. One problem that's really important to me is:

_____
_____
_____
_____
_____
_____
_____

I care about this because:

_____
_____
_____
_____
_____
_____
_____
_____

Here's what I do to try to make it better:

_____
_____
_____
_____
_____
_____
_____

I also think some things in the world have gotten much better since I was a kid. One thing that's gotten better is:

_____

_____

_____

_____

_____

It got better because:

_____

_____

_____

_____

_____

_____

That's important to me because:

_____

_____

_____

_____

_____

_____

_____

Here's some more stuff I want to tell you about feelings:

# More About Me Now

I hope I've told you most of what you want to know about what things are like while I'm looking forward to you being born. I probably missed a few things, and that's okay—don't forget, you can always ask me questions about anything you want to know. I do have a few other important points I haven't mentioned yet, though! Here's the rest of what you need to know about life right before you.

My favorite animal is: _____

Here's what I like about it:

_____

_____

_____

_____

_____

_____

_____

_____

_____

_____

_____

_____

_____

_____

_____

_____

_____

☐   I would want one to live with me.

☐   I would not want one to live with me.

☐   I have one who lives with me!

The most interesting cool true fact I know is:

_____

_____

_____

_____

_____

_____

_____

_____

The most interesting cool not-true fact I just made up is:

_____

_____

_____

_____

_____

_____

_____

_____

_____

_____

Here's a recipe for something I can cook or bake:

My favorite color is: _____

Here are some things I own that are my favorite color:

☐ Car

☐ Bedspread

☐ Jacket

☐ Shoes

☐ Bag

☐ Hair

☐ Other: _____

But I really don't like this color: _____

Maybe I don't like it because:

_____

_____

_____

_____

_____

_____

_____

# Wait, there's some other stuff I haven't told you yet!

# 3.

# With You

You'll like this part of the book, because you're in it! (That's why I like it, too.) Remember, when I'm writing this for you, you aren't here yet—but I've been spending a lot of time preparing for your arrival and thinking about what life will be like with a new beloved person around. It's going to be very different, and also a lot of fun! So let's talk about what life will be like together.

Here's a drawing I made of our family with you in it!
(I used my imagination.)

# Looking Forward to You

Sometimes when a kid joins a family, it's the result of a lot of planning and effort, and other times it's almost a surprise. But no matter what the backstory is, a new family addition is exciting and a little bit scary. It's hard to know for sure what to expect, but here's a little about what I think we'll do and how we'll grow together.

☐  I always knew I wanted kids.

☐  I learned I wanted kids pretty recently.

Here's the story of how you joined my family:

_____

_____

_____

_____

_____

_____

_____

_____

_____

_____

_____

_____

_____

_____

_____

_____

_____

_____

_____

_____

_____

_____

_____

When I was little I thought I'd name my kid:

We almost named you:

Here's why we chose your name instead:

When you get here, I'm most excited about:

I'm most nervous about:

I'm pretty sure you will:

_____
_____
_____
_____
_____
_____
_____

But I'm pretty sure you won't:

_____
_____
_____
_____
_____
_____
_____

And I'd be VERY surprised if you:

_____
_____
_____
_____
_____
_____
_____

You're going to have so many grown-ups who love you! Here's how many special grown-ups I think will be in your life:

_____ moms

_____ dads

_____ grandparents

_____ aunts

_____ uncles

_____ grown-up friends

_____ teachers

_____ other: _____

And can you believe every one of those grown-ups *also* has feelings and stories and favorites, just like me (and you)? If you're curious, you can ask them some of the same questions in this book!

I can't wait to share these with you:

Books:

_____
_____
_____
_____
_____
_____

Movies:

_____
_____
_____
_____
_____
_____

Hobbies:

_____
_____
_____
_____
_____
_____

Games:

_____

_____

_____

_____

Places:

_____

_____

_____

_____

Traditions:

_____

_____

_____

_____

Other:

_____

_____

_____

_____

_____

Here's a bedtime story I wrote for you before you existed:

# Advice
# for You

I don't know everything. You'll find that out soon, if you don't know it already. Sometimes, you might even think I know nothing at all! (It's okay to feel that way sometimes, although you still have to listen to me.) But I've been around a pretty long time, and I also care a lot about helping you be the happiest, bravest, most curious and content person you can be. Here are a few things I've learned that might help—we can try them out together!

Here are some things I've learned about how to have good relationships with other people (your family, your friends, your community, even me!):

_____

_____

_____

_____

_____

_____

_____

_____

_____

Here are some things I've learned about how to feel good about the regular things you do every day, like your job and your chores at home:

_____

_____

_____

_____

_____

_____

_____

_____

_____

Here are some things I've learned about how to feel as good as possible in your body:

_____
_____
_____
_____
_____
_____
_____
_____
_____
_____

Here are some things I've learned about how to keep your brain moving and growing:

_____
_____
_____
_____
_____
_____
_____
_____
_____
_____
_____

Here are some things I think you should know that don't fit in any of those categories:

_____
_____
_____
_____
_____
_____
_____
_____
_____
_____
_____

Here's a quote from someone else that I think is good advice:

_____
_____
_____
_____
_____
_____
_____
_____
_____
_____
_____
_____

# Your Questions for Me

I wrote all of this before I met you, but now you're here and reading this, and maybe you have questions! What do you want to know about that I didn't already write down? Let's talk about your questions together.

These pages are extra space for more questions and anything else I didn't have room for!

YOUR QUESTIONS FOR ME